let's travel in
FRANCE

Edited by Darlene Geis

A TRAVEL PRESS BOOK

PICTURE ACKNOWLEDGMENTS
The illustrations in this book are the work of the following photographers and artists, whose collaboration is gratefully acknowledged. For the full-color pictures, Pan-American Airways (1); P.I.P. Photos, in co-operation with Réalités (2, 3, 5, 6, 7, 8, 10, 11, 12, 13, 14, 15, 17, 18, 19, 20, 21, 22, 23, 25, 26, 27, 29, 30, 31, 32); Forbert, from Shostal (4); Nadelmann, from FPG (9); J. R. Johnson, of Rapho-Guillumette (16); Muench, from APA (24); Orville Goldner (28). For the black-and-white photographs we wish to thank the French Government Tourist Office; Jon Schults and George Daniell, from Photo Researchers, Inc.; Curtis Reider and Robert Cohen, from Black Star; Henri Cartier-Bresson, David Seymour, Sergio Larrain, Robert Capa, from Magnum; Brassai, from Rapho-Guillumette; P.I.P. Photos, in co-operation with Réalités; Orville Goldner. The map was made by Enrico Arno. The black-and-white art is from the Bettmann Archive. Designed by Helen Lewis (Sudler & Hennessey).

7 8 9 10 11 12 13 14 15 16 17 18 19 20 21 22 23 24 25   R   75 74 73 72 71 70 69 68 67

CONTENTS

GREAT BRITAIN

ENGLISH CHANNEL

NORMANDY

ATLANTIC OCEAN

Rouen

18

1-13 Paris

Seine

14

Versailles

Mont-Saint-Michel

19

15 16

St-Malo

Chartres

17

21

Fontainebleau

20

BRITTANY

BURG

Loire River

22

32

PARIS

9-10

11

Blvd. Clichy

Av. de Wagram

Blvd. Haussmann

Rue de la Fayette

8

Av. Kleber

Champs Elysées

Avenue F.D.R.

Rue de l'Opéra

Rue de Rivoli

R. Montmartre

Blvd. de Sébastopol

Bordeaux

7

12 13

2-3

Quai d'Orsay

4

6

5

Blvd. St. Germain

Rocamadour

Garonne River

Carcassonne

24

GASCONY

SPAIN

PYRENEES

23

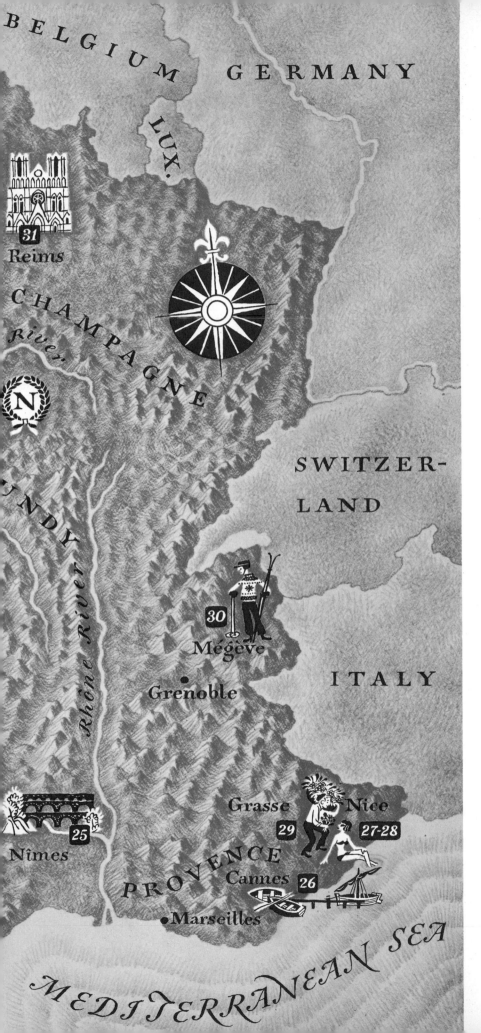

Locales of thirty-two full-page pictures

FRANCE, THE LAND OF ENCHANTMENT

T WO loves have I, my own country and France." This refrain has been the theme song of millions of enchanted tourists in the years since World War I.

And no wonder! The star-shaped country, stretching its points in all directions, is certainly the most glittering and glamorous one on the entire map of Europe. A look at that map shows us that France has unusual geographic advantages. She is the bridge between northern Europe and the Mediterranean world to the south. A narrow channel of water separates her from cool, green England to the north, and a not very wide sea, the Mediterranean, lies between her and Africa, whose hot winds blow across her southern shores.

Besides these neighbors she shares common borders with six other countries—Spain, Italy, Switzerland, Germany, Luxembourg and Belgium. It is not surprising, then, that for centuries France was the dominant influence, the "center" of Europe's civilization.

What *is* surprising is that this country covers only 213,000 square miles, and is 50,000 square miles *smaller* than the state of Texas! Yet within the French borders lie the sunny Riviera, snow-covered Alps, some of the world's greatest vineyards, an enviable system of navigable rivers, industrial cities, and enough fertile farmland to feed France's 42,000,000 people.

The brilliant heart of this star-shaped land is its capital, Paris, the City of Light. Paris lies well to the north of central France, but the country

The boat-shaped Ile de la Cité was once all of Paris. Now it is its quiet heart.

grew and radiated from it, and historically the core of France is Paris. How it expanded into the country we know today is a fascinating story.

PARIS, INCOMPARABLE CITY

It all started on a tiny island in the middle of the Seine (SAYN) River, over 2,000 years ago. A tribe of pagan fishermen lived there, and, in his chronicles of the conquest of Gaul, as France was then called, Julius Caesar wrote about them in 53 B.C. He called their island Lutetia (*loo*-TEE-*shi-ah*) and the people, Parisii (*pah*-RIZ-*ih-ee*). Centuries later, when the community had spread to the riverbanks on either side of the island, it borrowed its name from these early people and was known as Paris.

From the very first there was a special feeling about Paris. Attila the Hun spared it when he and his barbarian horde overran the rest of Gaul. And the early French kings chose it as their capital city. Charles V put it into words when he said, "Other cities are towns; Paris is a world."

That feeling has persisted down to this very day. Who does not experience a lifting of the heart at the prospect of visiting Paris? The city itself is beautiful—pearly gray buildings laced with green parks and broad tree-shaded streets and, winding through its center, the silvery Seine spanned by 32 graceful bridges. Its colorful history is written in every street and quarter. But though the past is everywhere at hand, the city lives for now. The present is vivid, and the practical Parisian improves his shining hours with pleasant living and a keen awareness of the current state of affairs.

The small boat-shaped island from which the city sprang still rides at anchor, moored to the riverbanks by eight bridges. Today it is called the Ile de la Cité (EEL *duh lah see*-TAY), and where an ancient pagan altar once stood, the Gothic glory of Notre Dame de Paris (NOH-*truh* DAHM *duh pah*-REE) now rises.

10

The left bank of the Seine is today, as it has been since the Middle Ages, the section of Paris devoted to learning. It is here that we find Paris the university town, famed for its serious scholars as well as for its prankish students. The Right Bank is dedicated to commerce, the world of fashion, theaters, palaces and the artists' quarter of Montmartre (mon-MAR-tr). Throughout the city there are innumerable small "quarters," each with a distinct flavor and a personality of its own. Paris, like the rest of France, is made up of individuals, none of whom lose their essential character in becoming part of the whole. Perhaps that is what charms the visitor most.

THE ILE-DE-FRANCE, HEART OF THE COUNTRY

Just as Paris grew in widening circles around the nucleus of the Ile de la Cité, so France grew in spreading rings around Paris, one province at a time. The region immediately surrounding Paris is known by the old name of "Ile-de-France" (EEL-*duh*-FRAHNSS). Actually it *is* almost an island, nearly surrounded by rivers.

In the old days the Ile-de-France, with Paris at its center, was all of France. Hugh Capet, whose kingdom this was a thousand years ago, could mount his horse and ride around his little country in a single day. And today the tourist can make side trips from Paris within a few hours' time to see the wonders of the Ile-de-France that surround it. There is the magnificent palace of Versailles (*vair*-SIGH) to the west; the village of Chartres (SHAHR-*tr*), with its glorious cathedral, to the southwest; Barbizon, with its landscapes beloved by painters, and the nearby palace of Fontainebleau (FON-*t'n-blow*), to the south; and Saint-Denis (*sahn*-D'NEE), where the kings of France are buried, to the north.

From this heartland of France, the country spread out to her present boundaries. Many of her provinces were settled by other peoples; some were founded years earlier than the Ile-de-France. All have added their special flavor and color to the country. Going counterclockwise around the Ile-de-France, we will visit some of the better-known provinces and sample the variety that adds up to *La Belle France*.

NORMANDY, PROVINCE OF CONQUERORS

The country along the English Channel to the north and west of Paris was settled by the Vikings centuries ago. Today, Normandy is renowned for its architecture, its apples and its great seaports. If you come to France by ship, you will probably debark at Cherbourg (SHARE-*boor*) or Le Havre (*luh* HAH-*vr*), and the boat train will take you through the picturesque Norman countryside. There you will see neat green fields, sleek cows, apple orchards in profusion, and the steep-roofed houses typical of

Normandy. Unfortunately, many of the most beautiful villages of Normandy have not yet recovered from the devastation of World War II.

Rouen (*roo*-AHN), where Joan of Arc was burned at the stake, is the chief city of Normandy. Calvados (*kahl-vah*-DOS), a powerful brandy made from all those apples, is the favorite tipple. And sea food and superb dairy products combine to make the fine regional dishes of this province.

BRITTANY, RUGGED SEA-DASHED SHORES

The westernmost point of the French star is Brittany. You cannot see its bare and rockbound coast jutting out into the Atlantic without being reminded of other coastlines that have bred a group of men who like many of the Bretons are great fishermen and sailors. Jacques Cartier sailed from the Breton coast on his voyage of discovery up the St. Lawrence River. Brittany was settled by a group of venturesome seafarers who sailed to its rocky shores from what are now the British Isles. Traces of their Celtic background can be seen in Brittany to this day.

BORDEAUX, NOBLE WINE COUNTRY

There are three great wine-growing areas in France—Bordeaux (*bore*-DOUGH), Burgundy and Champagne—and each produces a distinctive grape and wine. On the west coast and pointing down towards Spain

The vines have tender grapes, and before the crop is bottled young Frenchmen get their share.

is the Bordeaux section. Here in the valley of the Garonne (*ga*-RON) River the neat vineyards spread in rows under the hot sun. Each vineyard belongs to a castle and each produces a special wine. And these princely wines are the aristocrats of the table. This section, from Bordeaux to the Pyrenees, is the land of rich food and drink. Aside from its wines, it produces Armagnac (*ar-mah*-NYAHK) brandy, truffles and goose liver in abundance, as well as cheese and the most famous hams in France.

THE PYRENEES, FRANCE'S SOUTHWESTERN WALL

The Pyrenees form the wild mountain borderland that holds France and Spain apart. A rugged and fascinating country, this is the home of the Basque (BASK) people. They speak their own language, have games and dances peculiarly their own, and yet the Basques are loyally French. This is another example of the striking individuality to be found among the people of this land.

In the foothills of the Pyrenees prehistoric caves have been discovered. These, and some larger caves farther north, are the earliest time capsules of the human race, with records painted on the cave walls telling what life was like 15,000 years ago. Another cave or grotto near the mountains is of special interest, too. It is the grotto where a vision of the Virgin Mary was seen by a little peasant girl of Lourdes, who later became Saint Bernadette.

THE SOUTH OF FRANCE, GOLDEN PLAYGROUND

The south of France is warm and fragrant and vivid. Arles (ARL), where Van Gogh (*van* GO) painted, has the brilliance of his color dyed into the skies and fields and trees. And winding from the great seaport of Marseilles (*mar*-SAY) to the Italian border is that incredible strand of pleasure resorts known as the Riviera.

To the north, near the Swiss border, is a quite different resort area. Here the sun seems paler as it flashes on the white snow of the Alps, and bikinis have been replaced by ski suits. But the mountain scenery around Mont Blanc (*mon* BLAHN) needs no help from bathing beauties.

BURGUNDY AND CHAMPAGNE, WHERE
THE GRAPE IS KING

Between Mont Blanc and Paris lies the old, once powerful duchy of Burgundy. Today it is mostly given over to the cultivation of grapes and the bottling of the rich wines that bear its name. The famous flinty slopes of the Côte d'Or (COAT DOOR), where numerous vineyards thrive, belonged to monasteries in the old days, and monks did most of the wine making.

Farther north, and not far to the east of Paris, is Reims (RANSS), chief city of the province of Champagne. The great cathedral, where for 700 years nearly every French king was crowned, has been reconstructed since its near ruin in World War I. Beneath the city are the famous underground champagne cellars, chalk caves where the sparkling wine is aged. These cellars hold one of the great riches of France, for champagne, which comes from just a small region right outside Reims, is shipped all over the world.

13

THE SPIRIT OF FRANCE

This beautiful country has been blessed spiritually as well as physically. France is a nation of independent thinkers and, though she is famous for exports of wine, perfume and other luxuries, she has also exported more than her fair share of ideas. The philosophers Descartes (*day*-CART) and Rousseau (*roo*-SO), the writers Voltaire (*vol*-TAIR), Flaubert (*flow*-BARE) and Proust (PROOST) influenced thinking and writing far beyond the borders of France. Within the past century, the world has benefited from the scientific work of Pasteur (*pahss*-TUR) and Madame Curie, and we have seen modern painting take entirely new directions under the influence of Monet (*mo*-NAY), Matisse (*mah*-TEESS), Cézanne (*say*-ZAN) and the many other men of genius who have raised French art to the greatest heights ever.

France's cultural leadership, her rich resources, her record as a self-supporting agrarian nation, with a people skilled in handicrafts, do not count for as much in the highly industrialized twentieth century as they used to. The Frenchman's passion for individuality makes him unwilling to become part of a mechanized society. He is not the type to regulate his

This little pig will go to table, the culinary masterpiece of an artistic chef.

life by the blasts of a factory whistle. Fundamentally, the Frenchman is an artist. He is an artist about the products he makes, the fruits and vegetables he grows, the food he prepares. But above all he is an artist in his way of life. Perhaps it is that artistry we most admire and try to emulate when we visit France. Governments may fall and Premiers may come and go. The Frenchman still lives with grace and style. There is nothing more instructive than to sit at a sidewalk café and observe how he does it. And that is just what we are going to do next.

let's travel in
FRANCE

OUTDOOR CAFE: THE CHAMPS ELYSEES

ONE of the first moves a tourist makes in Paris—after cashing a traveler's check —is to amble out onto the broad sidewalks, find an outdoor café and give himself over to the enjoyment of *la vie parisienne*. The sidewalk cafés are seldom empty in this city, where the tempo is leisurely and people have time to take pleasure in what they are doing.

Look westward up the wide and beautiful Champs Elysées (*shan zay-lee*-ZAY) toward the Arc de Triomphe (ARK *duh tree*-OMF). This broad thoroughfare came into existence only after the time of Napoleon. Before that the "Elysian Fields" stretched to the west as far as the eye could see. These green fields were the market gardens and poultry farms that supplied Paris with most of her food. As late as 1800 only six houses intruded on the landscape. But when Napoleon began the building of the impressive Arc de Triomphe, the city spread westward toward it. Now this is one of the most fashionable sections in all of Paris.

Along this stretch of the Champs Elysées there are movie theaters, elegant shops and some of the smartest cafés in the city. Since the war, the French motion picture industry has become established in this district. And stars and celebrities are to be seen here in their natural habitat. Nevertheless, it is the habitat itself, Paris, that gets top billing.

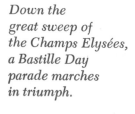

Down the great sweep of the Champs Elysées, a Bastille Day parade marches in triumph.

PANORAMA OF PARIS: VIEW FROM NOTRE DAME

OUR strange-looking companion to the right has been grinning down on this marvelous city for about 100 years. He is one of the famous gargoyles of Notre Dame, but though the cathedral dates back to the twelfth century, this Gothic oddity was added just about a hundred years ago when Notre Dame was restored. Actually these grotesque creatures serve a useful purpose. They are decorative waterspouts through whose open mouths the rain water that collects in the roof gutters can run out.

From the tower of Notre Dame, 387 steps above the little island from which Paris sprang, the city can be viewed in all its splendor. There below us is the Seine, a winding band of pewter. Its bridges are sturdy yet graceful, and no two of them are alike. We are facing west, and to our left is—but of course!—the Left Bank. In the distance you can see the Eiffel (EYE-*fel*) Tower, thrusting upward like an exclamation point above the quiet gray city. This is the trademark of Paris.

The golden dome just to the left of the tower crowns the largest building of a group known as the Hôtel des Invalides (*on-vah*-LEED). Originally built by Louis XIV as a sort of de luxe old soldier's home,

At cafés like this, Existentialism was born. Fast cars and philosophy are the hobbies of the Left Bank jet set.

the Invalides is now primarily a museum of France's military glory. But its chief claim to fame is that under the golden dome rest the mortal remains of one Napoleon Bonaparte.

Though the view is superb, we cannot stay up here on the tower of Notre Dame any longer, because all of Paris is waiting for us below.

NOTRE DAME CATHEDRAL: GOTHIC MASTERPIECE

DESCENDING to the Ile de la Cité, we cross one of the little bridges behind the cathedral and pause on the Left Bank to gaze back at one of the marvels of Paris.

Seen from this vantage point, Notre Dame appears to float on the river, almost lightly. The genius of Gothic architecture at its best—and Notre Dame is a prime example—was its ability to give enormously heavy masonry the look of lightness. Arches soar, carved stone resembles lace, and here the flying buttresses which support the walls of the cathedral really seem to fly, they appear so weightless.

Notre Dame was begun in 1163 and finished about a hundred years later. That was long before the days of structural steel. But the artists who built in those days were carried along on the great tide of religious fervor that swept Europe. They performed miracles in stone. Somehow they managed to translate man's spiritual striving into the vaulting arches of masonry. We read their message today in the great cathedrals they created so long ago.

The walls of Notre Dame are exceptionally thick—a carry-over from Romanesque architecture. As a result, the windows do not give much light, and it is one of the darkest of the great cathedrals. But its glorious stained glass windows filter a kind of subdued rainbow shimmer into the shadowy interior. In this view you can see one of the remarkable rose windows about midway along the side of the cathedral. Some of its glass is still the original twelfth-century stained glass, irreplaceable because no one today can duplicate those gemlike fragments.

Unlike the rivers of most great cities, the Seine retains a country atmosphere, especially along the shores that flow past this quiet old island. There are always hopeful fishermen angling along the banks, but no one has ever seen them catch anything.

BROWSING AT
THE BOOKSTALLS:
ALONG THE
LEFT BANK

RUNNING along both banks of the Seine are the *Quais* (KAY), or masonry embankments. These were built originally as a mooring place for the river traffic that has played such a large part in the fortunes of Paris. For if Paris is the heart of France, then the Seine is her main artery, carrying produce and goods from the countryside to the capital, and in return bringing the products of the city to the other parts of France.

Along the broad parapets of the Left Bank the dealers in second-hand books and old prints have set up shop in a series of hinged wooden boxes. This riverside promenade is conducive to rambling walks and idle browsing, and the owners of the bookstalls engage in a flourishing, if fair-weather, business. In this picture we are just across the river from the Louvre (LOOVR), the famous art museum, and you can see one of its stately wings rising beyond the end of the bridge.

It is on the Left Bank of the river that we find the Latin Quarter, which got its name back in the thirteenth century. Even then the section abounded in universities, and there were 15,000 students living in the quarter. All of them spoke the language of the learned—Latin—so this section was called the Pays Latin (*pay-EE lah-TAN*), or the Latin Country. Because of student high jinks down through the ages, the Latin Quarter now has a rather raffish reputation.

Printers, bookbinders and booksellers are located in this section near the universities, a logical and practical arrangement that enhances the intellectual atmosphere of the Left Bank. The august French Academy, that most exclusive institution of France's literary greats, is located near the *quais*. Its forty "Immortals" meet every Thursday, and it was these men who started the vogue of rummaging through the riverside bookstalls. One wonders what the "Immortals" bought one-half so precious as the things they wrote.

THE EIFFEL TOWER:
SYMBOL
OF PARIS

LET us stroll along the Left Bank until we reach the Eiffel Tower. It rises above us strikingly photogenic, a magnet for camera-happy tourists in search of the perfect souvenir of Paris. Soaring more than 900 feet above the low roofs of the city, this metal tower was built for an exposition held in Paris in 1889.

The Parisians thought it was a monstrously ugly blot on their landscape, and for years people have been agitating to have it torn down. But the spire, which looks as though it were made from a giant Erector set, has become a world-famous landmark, and one of the favorite tourist attractions of Paris. An elevator takes us to the balcony near the top, and though some people get a bit woozy from the sway of the tower, they are rewarded with a spectacular view of Paris and the surrounding countryside.

About a million and a half people a year are drawn to the Eiffel Tower, and the man who operates it on a concession from the city has made it a profitable enterprise. On the lowest and largest level he has even built a fine luxury restaurant—for those who like to live high without having to go all the way to the top of the tower.

The Paris police wear their dashing uniform in typical French style.

25

FOOD FOR A GOURMET: THE ART OF FRENCH COOKING

THE food of France is justly famous, and the men who prepare and cook it are practitioners of a high art. Their dishes are created to delight the eye as well as the palate, and at the right we see a still life worthy of a great painter, made up of the "fruits of the sea" which the chef will use in a hearty bouillabaisse (*boo-yah*-BASE), or fish chowder.

Every section of France has developed its own special cuisine. Burgundy, for example, excels in dishes cooked in the red wine of the region, strong and savory. Lyonnais (*lee-oh*-NAY) is known for its country fare—sausages, fritters, and potatoes fried with onions. Provence (*pro*-VAHNSS), in the sun-baked south, is famous for its Mediterranean cuisine, hot and spicy with olive oil, garlic, anchovies, pimentos, eggplant and all the riches of the sea.

We have gone to one of the renowned eating places on the Left Bank that specializes in Provençal cuisine. It is called Le Relais de Porquerolles (*luh ruh*-LAY *duh por*-KROLL), and one whiff of the steamy fragrance of its bouillabaisse and you think you are in the south of France. This broth, golden with saffron, spiced with garlic, has in it every kind of fish and sea food found in the Mediterranean. Generally it is served only on Fridays—good enough reason for that to be a special day on any gourmet's calendar.

Chefs and wine stewards are delighted to offer their superlative best for the critical connoisseur.

26

EVENING IN PARIS: PLACE DE LA CONCORDE

THERE is no more impressive spot for crossing over from the Left Bank to the Right than at the Place de la Concorde (PLAHSS *duh lah kon*-KORD). And at night it is beautiful beyond belief. Here is city planning at its most dramatic, and when we look at the spaciousness and balance of the Place de la Concorde we realize that cities don't achieve beauty by accident.

This enormous square was designed over 200 years ago by the architect of Louis XV, the king who said, "After me, the deluge." Little did he dream that the most horrible aspect of the deluge was to take place in his beautiful square. For it was here that the guillotine was set up, and here that Louis's luckless grandson, Louis XVI, and his wife, Marie Antoinette, were beheaded before a gleeful Paris mob. In an effort to cleanse the square of its bloody associations, the Parisians later named it the Place de la Concorde.

We see it here at the magic hour of nightfall, with the hill of Montmartre spangled with lights in the background, and the white towers of Sacré-Coeur (SAH-*kray*-KUR) rising above the city in ghostly radiance. The Egyptian Obelisk of Luxor marks the center of the Place, and around it you can see the streaming lights of the traffic that swirls through this busy square. The long buildings facing us are, to the right, the Admiralty and, to the left, the Automobile Club and the famous Hôtel Crillon (*kree*-YOHN). The street that cuts between them is the Rue Royale (ROO *rwa*-YAHL), and at its head is the Greek-pillared Madeleine Church.

All the brilliance and sparkle of Paris are caught in this nocturnal scene. On Sundays and holidays the obelisk becomes a shaft of light and the classic buildings are dramatically illuminated. Fountains play their silvery jets, and the Place de la Concorde is a symphony of light and sound. At such moments there are few visitors who do not succumb to the beauty of this City of Light and love it forever after.

BUSIEST SPOT
IN PARIS:
PLACE DE L'OPERA

A SHORT way behind the Madeleine Church is the Place de l'Opéra (PLAHSS *duh low-pay-*RAH), where boulevards and people converge to make one of the busiest spots in Paris.

The imposing Opéra itself was built nearly a hundred years ago and reflects the ornate elegance of the Second Empire, when Empress Eugénie set the styles. On gala nights the Opéra is ablaze with the brilliance of its own décor and the fabulous gowns, jewels, uniforms and medals of its audience. Some of its critics complain that it was built to show off its audience rather than the music, for its acoustics are poor and several hundred seats have no view of the stage whatsoever. However, the Opéra is subsidized by the Republic of France, and as a result tickets are priced moderately enough so that even the better seats are not expensive.

Some of the most famous cafés in Paris are concentrated around the Opéra. Best known among them is the familiar Café de la Paix (*kah-*FAY *duh lah* PAY). This has long been a favorite meeting place of Americans in Paris, probably because the indispensable American Express is nearby. Also, the Rue de la Paix, with its tempting shops, leads the weary almost to the door of the café that bears its name. Parisians' homes are private, but the people enjoy mingling in the life of their city. So the tradition of the sidewalk café was born, and it is one of the most endearing that Paris has to offer to its visitors.

The Grand Staircase of the Paris Opéra was designed to set off magnificence.

30

SQUARE IN MONTMARTRE: THE ARTISTS' QUARTER

HERE we are in one of the most charming sections of Paris. We have climbed about halfway up the hill of Montmartre, and now we stand on one of the narrow streets just below the white dome of Sacré-Coeur. The basilica was built on the summit of the Hill of the Martyr, or Montmartre, where St. Denis was put to death in the third century when he tried to convert the Parisians to Christianity. The Hill of the Martyr has undergone a good many changes since those pagan times.

A hundred years ago Montmartre was a village. In those quaint old days—actually not so long ago—there were windmills gently revolving up on this hill. The little houses and gardens belonged to farmers and working people, and very few outsiders ventured the steep climb.

But around the turn of the century artists and writers, blessed with youth and vitality if not with worldly goods, climbed the hill in search of cheap lodgings. They found that old barns and shanties made wonderful studios and that village life could be charmingly spiked with a dash of Bohemianism. So the artists' quarter got its start. Some of the great artists who lived here—Toulouse-Lautrec (*too*-LOOZ-*low*-TREK), Picasso, Utrillo (*you*-TRILL-*oh*)—immortalized the old Montmartre in their early canvases. Today this section of Paris is still sitting for its portrait by new young painters.

One of the busiest places in Montmartre is the Place du Tertre (PLAHSS *du* TAIRTR), a little square that used to be the center of village life. These days tables and chairs are crowded under bright umbrellas and under the trees. The cafés where villagers once gossiped have been taken over by visitors. But the small-town informality of the old times still prevails, and this village square is a pleasant oasis in the big city.

OLD MASTER
OF MONTMARTRE:
OUTDOOR PAINTER

ORDINARILY, when we think of artists in Paris we think of gay young blades studying art, living on hope, and leading a colorful and irresponsible existence. But artists don't stay young any more than the rest of us do. And some of the youths of 1910 are still around Montmartre in the service of their muse.

This bearded painter might well have spent long-ago evenings roistering with the young Picasso and other hopeful artists. Some of them went on to fame, and some just kept on painting at the same old stand. And there were probably others who gave up when they realized they didn't have the divine spark.

But here is a man who stayed with art in spite of meager rewards. He obviously loves what he is doing, and that is reward enough. You can see painters like this on nearly every street and square of Montmartre. Day after day, year in, year out, they have tried to capture the look of their enchanting city on canvas. Sometimes they are lucky, and a passing tourist buys one of their paintings and carries it off to hang on the wall of a neat and proper living room in Kansas or Saskatchewan. Sometimes the going is rough, but the little bars and restaurants will extend credit during the lean days. The artist seems always to have faith that what he is doing will be appreciated eventually. He knows that priceless canvases by Gauguin (go-GAN) and Van Gogh, for example, went begging for years while the artists lived from hand to mouth.

So this fellow with the serene and happy face goes on painting against all odds. He doesn't care if Fame comes a little late. He will sit at his easel waiting patiently for her, confident that she doesn't mean to stand him up altogether. In the meantime, though, he doesn't dare to be extravagant with materials. His canvases, you will notice, are quite small.

MOKAREX
Formfit
IVE LES
AMERICAS
FILTER
COGNAC POLIGNAC
MOULIN ROUGE
LIN ROUGE
TABAC
TABAC
CYRANO

THE MOULIN ROUGE: GAY NIGHT LIFE

THE Gay Paree of night lights and entertainment exists mainly as a tourist attraction.

Here is the Boulevard Clichy (*bool*-VAR *klee*-SHE), burning brightly to attract all the gay moths in the neighborhood. Nearby is the notorious Place Pigalle (PLAHSS *pee*-GAHL), affectionately known as "Pig Alley" to hundreds of American boys during World War II.

The mills of Montmartre *did* have a reputation for fun and games many years ago. They were used as dance halls at night by the serving maids and working men who lived in the quarter. Then the artists took over, and the entertainment became more sophisticated.

Not all of Paris is a city of night lights and gay entertainment. Les Halles, covering many square blocks off the right bank of the Seine, is a wholesale market that is a beehive of activity.

Many small farms around the city provide fresh food for the whole of Paris. During the night and early morning hours the farmers bring their wares to Les Halles which is part of the tradition of Paris. An early morning visit to this bustling market is fascinating and rewarding.

Les Halles has been threatened in recent years with replacement by smaller and more efficient markets, but many Parisians are reluctant to give up an institution that is part of the flavor of their gourmet city. The teeming market survives and farmers and fishermen continue to gather there.

Les Halles, "the belly of Paris," is heaped with fresh food for a gourmet city.

PALACE OF ART: THE LOUVRE AND GARDENS

WE ARE standing in the great courtyard of the Louvre, enclosed on three sides by its massive gray buildings. At the open end the Arc de Triomphe du Carrousel (*kah-roo-*SELL) commemorates the victories of Napoleon. The year 1806 was a proud one for the Little Corporal, for that was the year he had this victory arch and the more famous one on the Champs Elysées begun. Both were completed after his death, however, and this arch is now surmounted by a bronze chariot group that represents the Restoration of the Bourbon kings. The kings, too, are gone, but the arch remains, set like a gateway between the gardens of the Tuileries (TWEEL-*ree*) and the Place du Carrousel.

The formal gardens look like an enormous outdoor room carpeted with a patterned rug of living plants. One of the most popular attrac-

One of the best-loved figures in French history was Joan of Arc, the militant peasant girl, burned at the stake and proclaimed a saint.

tions of the Tuileries is the large "Round Pond," where Parisian children sail their toy boats. But for grown-ups the gray buildings of the Louvre exert a stronger pull.

Kings, emperors and the Republic have added to this enormous palace, and now it is almost a city within a city, with one long wing running parallel to the Seine and another stretching for blocks along the Rue de Rivoli (ROO *duh ree-vo-*LEE). We are going inside, but in one visit to the Louvre we can scarcely expect to do more than scratch the surface.

ROMAN ANTIQUITIES: GALLERY IN THE LOUVRE

ALMOST the entire history of France could be told in terms of the great building which we have now entered. In the thirteenth century King Philip Augustus built a fortified dungeon where he could house his treasures while he went off on a Crusade. He put his wife, his wealth, his prisoners and his soldiers in the Louvre for safekeeping, and today the Louvre is still the repository for the great treasures of France.

It would take years to see all the art treasures of the world amassed in the forty acres of this fabulous palace. The Orient, Greece, Rome and Egypt are represented within these splendid rooms with the finest flowerings of their ancient civilizations. Through an arch we enter the galleries devoted to the statues and busts of the severe citizens of Imperial Rome. Their classic simplicity in cool white marble is an interesting contrast to the ornate and colorful style of a French palace.

Kings and queens once lived and moved in these spacious halls. The most famous gallery of all is the Grande Galerie (GRAHND *gal*-REE) on whose walls now hang what is perhaps the greatest concentration of masterpieces ever collected in one "room." It is here that you will find the most celebrated painting in the world, the *Mona Lisa*. But in the days when the Louvre housed the court, the kings of France used to hold audience in the Grande Galerie once a year. The monarch would walk down the long, long room, laying the royal hand on any subject suffering from scrofula, or the "king's evil," for it was believed that his touch was the cure for it.

When the kings of France lived in the Louvre, they were easily accessible to their people, and, for that reason, close to their hearts. But when Louis XIV moved his court ten miles out of Paris to Versailles, it was the beginning of the end of France's monarchy.

PALACE OF VERSAILLES: SPLENDID FRENCH COURT

VERSAILLES was nothing but a rude little village until King Louis XIII built a hunting lodge there. His son, Louis XIV, enlarged and elaborated on it, had the enormous parks and gardens laid out by the same man who planned the Tuileries Gardens; even the village was rebuilt. Versailles became the most magnificent royal palace in the world. It became, in fact, a glittering world in itself. The king and royal family lived there, as did hundreds of nobles and several thousand servants. In some respects their life was sumptuous and splendid beyond imagination. The palace floors, walls and ceilings are ornate and beautiful, and the furniture must have equaled them in gilded glory. But most of the artistic riches were carried off during the Revolution. The famous Hall of Mirrors, where the peace treaty of World War I was signed, looks like new, because much of Versailles has been restored—partly with the help of one million Rockefeller dollars.

Since 1953 many of the great palaces of France have been part of the fabulous Spectacles of Sound and Light, sponsored by the French government. At Versailles the Spectacle takes place four times a week—at night, of course. The palace, gardens and fountains are illuminated dramatically, and you can imagine this view—the great palace façade shining with golden lights while the statues around the Basin of Neptune are bathed in a green glow. Chairs are set up on the lawns for the large audiences, and speakers broadcast the history of glorious Versailles in stereophonic sound. André Maurois (*ahn*-DRAY *maw*-RWAH) and Jean Cocteau (ZHAHN *kawk*-TOE), two of France's most famous contemporary authors, wrote the script, and it was recorded by leading French actors.

42

CATHEDRAL
AND VILLAGE:
CHARTRES

IF VERSAILLES is one of the greatest palaces ever built for the glory of a king, the Cathedral of Notre Dame de Chartres is certainly one of the greatest edifices ever built for the glory of God. We see it majestically rising above the humble rooftops of the town of Chartres. The story is told that Our Lady chose this poor village and no other to grace with her most beautiful abode because she felt an affinity with the simple people.

In the thirteenth century religious fervor was running high. It was the time of the Crusades, when great kings and lords humbled themselves in the hope of achieving grace. When this cathedral was built, not only artisans and ordinary workmen labored on it. Nobles and royal princes came from miles around for the privilege of being yoked to the heavy blocks of stone at the quarry and then dragging them seven miles to the site of the cathedral.

In less than fifty years the unbelievable task of building and carving and making the stained glass windows was completed. No architect, sculptor or glazier signed his name to this community masterpiece. It had not been built for personal glory.

The cathedral is visited every year by thousands of people who come to marvel at the Gothic purity of its design. And not the least of its dramatic elements is the contrast between the stately Cathedral of Notre Dame and the humble town from which it sprang. The picture shows the contrast, with the elegant spires of the cathedral pointing to Heaven and the simple houses clustered modestly below.

STAINED GLASS WINDOW: GLORY OF CHARTRES

IN THIS picture we are in Chartres Cathedral looking at a panel of one of the great stained glass windows that are the glory of Chartres. This is the Passion Window, and shows the *Last Supper*.

The art of colored glass—it was not actually "stained" in the thirteenth century—came to Europe from the Far East. An intrinsic part of the design of the Gothic cathedrals was the high arch, or lancet, which was an open space in the heavy masonry, allowing for illumination. Because wall space was limited, the cathedral designers had to hang their colored decorations and religious pictures in these openings, and they solved the problem by doing them in colored glass.

Nothing has equaled the artistry of these glassmakers of the thirteenth and fourteenth centuries. Though modern techniques have improved the quality of the glass, we cannot duplicate their jewel-like colors and marvelous textures today.

The old master glaziers followed two main rules about their glass. First, they insisted on color as brilliant and vivid as they could make it. Second, an artist was judged by the quality of his blues. The blue glass could vary from a glowing sapphire to a luminous aquamarine. And it was the blue pieces in their relationship to the other colors that made the whole picture alive and vibrant. You can see the subtle range of blues in the *Last Supper* and notice how they give depth to what is really a flat picture.

This window is on the west façade of the cathedral, and when the afternoon sun pours through it, the colors blaze like some bright act of faith.

THE COURT
OF FAREWELLS:
PALACE OF
FONTAINEBLEAU

ALMOST on a straight line from Chartres to the east, and just south of Paris, is the second most popular chateau of France, Fontainebleau. Here you can see the imposing entrance, but because it was the scene of Napoleon's exit, it is called the Court of Farewells. In one of the rooms of Fontainebleau Napoleon was forced to sign his notice of abdication in 1814. With that stroke of the quill he gave up crown, throne, palace, even France itself. Before he was sent into exile on Elba, Napoleon stood in front of this very horseshoe staircase, and, with emotions running high, took leave of his old grenadier guards, companions in battle in his better days.

Fontainebleau was originally a hunting lodge. Kings Francis I and Henry II, both men of exceptional taste, imported Italian workmen and created one of the noblest architectural styles—French Renaissance. Henry II and his favorite, Diane de Poitiers (*dee*-AHN *duh pwah*-TYAY); Madame de Maintenon (*mant*-NOHN); Louis XV; Marie Antoinette; Napoleon and Josephine—all have left their personal mark on rooms or apartments which they occupied. Going through Fontainebleau is somewhat like taking a journey that brings you face to face with living French history.

Beautiful handwork is an old tradition in France, where each artisan takes pride in his skill.

49

FORTRESS OF RICHARD THE LIONHEARTED: NORMAN DUNGEON

LEAVING the Ile-de-France, we follow the Seine River to the northwest into Normandy. Just below Rouen, where the river meanders in looping curves through the rich farmlands, is the village of Le Petit Andely (*luh puh-*TEE *ahnd-el-*LEE). And brooding above the peaceful landscape we can see the ruins of Richard the Lionhearted's fortress, the Château Gaillard (*shah-*TOE *guy-*YAR).

Richard built this stronghold in 1196 to defend Normandy against the King of France. In a way the Château Gaillard symbolizes the tug-of-war between the kings of France and kings of England over this fruitful land. Richard had inherited the crown of England from his father and vast lands in France from his mother. He proposed to hang on to both.

Actually Normandy is very close to England, and invading armies have crossed the Channel both ways. The white chalk cliffs above the river here are the same natural formation as the cliffs of Dover. So there is even a geological relationship. But Normandy is part of France, and King Philip Augustus of France laid siege to Richard's castle and eventually regained Normandy for the French crown. The tough old fortress stood for four hundred years, during which time it was used as a dungeon for enemies of the court. We can only guess at the number of men and women who looked their last on this fair landscape and then were shut behind those grim walls, never to emerge again.

The quiet rivers wind through rich fields and changeless villages.

THE MAGIC
ISLAND:
MONT-SAINT-MICHEL

BETWEEN Normandy and Brittany, as we move westward, stands one of "The Marvels of the West," Mont-Saint-Michel (MOHN-*san-mee*-SHELL). As we see it now, reflected in the shallow water, it looms like an improbable fairy castle and village in the middle of nowhere.

This large cone-shaped rock rising out of a beach at one end of a bay has been inhabited since the days when Rome ruled Gaul. In the eighth century a chapel dedicated to Saint Michel was built on the rock. Later, in the thirteenth century, when miracles of construction were taking place all over France, a Gothic abbey was erected on the very summit of the rock. The abbey rose in three tiers, taking on the look of a make-believe castle. Because of its strategic position, it soon became a fortress as well as a place of religious pilgrimage, and defensive walls and towers were built around the base of the rock.

Little houses cling to the steep slopes between the walls below and the abbey above, and one narrow street lined with shops climbs to the peak. There is a mile-long causeway connecting Mont-Saint-Michel with the mainland. Trips to the Mont have to be carefully timed, for at low tide the seas recede to a distance of ten miles, but at high tide the waters come sweeping in to the base of the rock, and then Mont-Saint-Michel becomes an island.

The Mont is famous for its omelettes and is the home of the well-known restaurant of Madame Poulard, who is said to have invented the egg dish in the nineteenth century.

ICI HOTEL DE LA MERE POULARD
CE NOM TROP COMMUN AU MONT ST MICHEL
DOIT SA NOTORIÉTÉ MONDIALE A LA FONDATRICE DE CETTE MAISON
N'A PAS DE SUCCURSALE

This poster of Madame Poulard invites the hungry tourist to sample her omelettes.

BRETON FISHERMEN: BRINGING IN THE CATCH

THE peninsula of Brittany juts out into the wild Atlantic in a rocky, wind-swept point. In the old days, the Breton men were seafarers, fishing in distant waters, banding together as privateers to loot enemy merchant ships, and sailing on voyages of discovery. About 500 A.D. Brittany was settled by Britons who had been driven from their home island by the Anglo-Saxons. They sailed across the channel, bringing with them their Celtic language, folk tales and ancient customs.

Bretons still depend upon the sea for their main livelihood. In this picture we see one of the typical fishing villages that cling to the rocky inlets of this stern coast. From the larger port of Saint-Malo the fishing fleets sail to Newfoundland and Greenland every February. It will be autumn before they come back, and until then their women will pray for their safe return. But the women's hands will not be idle while they wait. Brittany is well-known for its beautiful lace, and for the pottery that comes from Quimper (*kam*-PAIR).

The food of this region is unusual and delicious. Sea food is prepared with the sauce called "Armorican," which gets its name from Armorica—the ancient name of Brittany. A wonderful rich cider, little buckwheat pancakes and *port-salut* cheese are the other regional specialties. Because it is such a picturesque part of France, Brittany is particularly popular with visitors.

The dock is deserted, except for two women watching for their fishermen's return.

SIMPLE PEASANT WOMAN: BRITTANY

BRITTANY is a "fairy-haunted land" of old beliefs and superstitions, and many of the familiar fairy tales and ancient legends—including those of King Arthur—had their origin here. Some of the Breton villages with their quaint, clean little cottages might have come right out of an illustration for an old storybook. The picture we are looking at now is a striking example.

It is not hard to imagine that this elderly peasant woman, sitting next to her high old-fashioned bed, might be waiting for a visit from her granddaughter, Red Ridinghood. Perhaps the granddaughter, dressed in her bright cloak and hood, is at this moment making her perilous way through the deep mysterious forest that covers parts of Brittany like a second sea. A number of the fairy tales that we all know supposedly took place in the enchanted forests of Brittany in the Middle Ages. We can thank the Bretons' stubborn clinging to tradition for letting us see today what their corner of France must have looked like six hundred years ago.

Oldsters in Brittany still dress in the national costume. The full-skirted, long black dress and the high, starched lace cap are a common sight on the village grandmothers. And the older men still wear their distinctive broad-brimmed hats—stylishly adapted for women by the Paris milliners and called "Breton sailors."

During the summer months Brittany is famous for its religious ceremonies known as "Pardons." Then young and old—even the littlest children—are dressed in the colorful Breton costumes. They march in long processions across the fields, singing hymns and carrying their holy banners to the local church. In this land of wild seacoast and haunted forest, where venturesome men pit themselves against the elements while brave women wait at home, religion is a strong and comforting part of life.

FLOATING
THROUGH FRANCE:
RIVER BARGE

THE star-shaped country of France is veined with rivers, and it is possible to travel from one end of the country to the other by means of these branching waterways. The Romans, though they were fanatic about building roads, were happy to use the rivers of France as their highways, too. Over the centuries the French have constructed canals, until now the rivers are linked in a system over 9,400 miles long.

Typical throughout the French countryside is this view of a quiet canal bordered by rows of poplars. The flat-bottomed barge moves dreamily along the smooth water carrying coal, petroleum or other freight, as well as the bargeman's family. Life aboard these boats may be cramped, but it must be fun! The barge people are a floating community, and the families all know one another and have many chances to get together when their boats are loading or unloading, or waiting to pass through the locks that are almost as numerous as crossroads on a highway.

The children have a special program of lessons and schooling, and although they may seem to live the life of water gypsies, the long arm of the French schoolteacher reaches even to these remote barges.

Canals and rivers link France with Belgium, Holland and Germany, and many vacationers, enviously observing the delightful life aboard the barges, have decided to travel through Europe by water, too. You can charter a flat-bottomed boat and meander through the pleasant countryside, stopping to explore the towns along the way. In France all water roads lead to Paris. The ultimate adventure would be to live aboard your boat in Paris, anchored along the *quais* of the Seine, with the merry barge community tied up nearby. Your tourist drip-dries would be in good company as they flapped on the washline strung above the deck. The family laundry takes the place of nautical pennants on these boats.

HARVESTING
THE GRAPES:
SOUTHERN
VINEYARD

TRAVELING down to the southwest of France, we come to the wild and mountainous province of the Pyrenees. From the Atlantic seaside resort of Biarritz (*bee-ah-*RITZ) to the Mediterranean, this province is the naturally fortified borderland between France and Spain. Suddenly we are in the warm and brilliant southern region near Perpignan (*pair-pee-*NYAHN). Here, unlike other sections of the Pyrenees, is land suitable for vineyards. Grapevines cannot thrive in the heavy black soil that nourishes luxuriant vegetation, so this sparse stony land is ideal for them.

You can see the flaming autumn colors of the vine leaves of these grapes that ripen late in this province of the Pyrenees. Whole families work in the vineyards harvesting the fragrant crop, filling their great baskets with heavy bunches of colorful grapes.

France is the greatest grape-growing country in the world. Something that cannot be duplicated elsewhere makes the soil in certain areas produce superlative grapes. Four million acres of land in France are devoted to this business that is a craft, a profession, almost a cult. The business and methods of growing grapes have been handed down from father to son for many generations. Most of the grapes grown in this sparse stony soil are used for making port. This product of the grape is a living thing to these people and must be handled with sensitivity, understanding and love.

The vineyards of the Pyrenees do not rank with the great vineyards of Bordeaux, Burgundy, Champagne, or even the Loire Valley. The aristocratic grapes that come from those sections of France are fruit for the gourmets, many of whom are such experts that they can pinpoint the very plot of ground that produced a certain fine type of grape. But you need not be an expert to enjoy the heady fragrance of the ripe grapes at harvest time, even in a modest vineyard.

MEDIEVAL WALLED CITY: CARCASSONNE

TRAVELING down from the Pyrenees toward the Mediterranean we seem suddenly to have left the twentieth century when we see Carcassonne (*kar-kah-*SUN) rise up before us like a fairytale castle. Knights in armor should come riding out of the gates, and ladies with caps as pointed as the towers should be standing at the battlements to wave good-by. But for the most part you will only meet other tourists on this path, or modern villagers going about their everyday affairs as though there were nothing unusual in living in this fabulous place that surpasses even Disneyland!

In medieval France there were many walled towns like Carcassonne, but most of them have fallen to the enemy—time. In the first century B.C., Carcassonne was a Roman military post. Six centuries later, the Visigoths built the first wall around the city. In the thirteenth century, the medieval walls that we see here were constructed. Carcassonne is surrounded by a double wall, crenelated and turreted so that, against the sky, it looks like a storybook city of old.

Knights of old rode off to the Crusades from walled cities like Carcassonne.

The River Aude (ODE) flows between the smaller walled city and the Lower Town, which spreads out unwalled upon the plain below. And that plain is like a sea of grapes. For it was here in the Mediterranean southland that early Greek travelers first planted vines and started the cultivation of the grape that France has continued so brilliantly.

62

OLD ROMAN AQUEDUCT: NIMES

AS FRANCE spread out from her northern capital, she embraced the provinces along the Mediterranean that had originally been part of the Roman Empire. So in the south of France we find cities that still retain landmarks of antiquity. The city of Nîmes (NEEM) is one of them. It was called "the Rome of Gaul" and it still has ruins of an amphitheater and a pillared Temple of Diana.

A wonderful sight is the magnificent Roman aqueduct called the Pont du Gard (PONE *doo* GAHR), or Bridge of the Gard River. It was built by order of Agrippa in 19 B.C. and carried water to Nîmes from a spring 25 miles away. Of all the marvelous aqueducts built by Roman ingenuity, the Pont du Gard in France is the finest example still remaining.

The upper tier of small arches supported the actual conduits that carried the water to Nîmes. Today a tourist center has sprung up near the Gard and its noble bridge. There are picnic grounds and concessions for souvenirs, food and drink. Paddle boats and rowboats can be rented, and a carnival atmosphere prevails in the shadow of Roman glory long since past. Not far from here is Avignon (*ah-veen-*YOHN), seat of the Papacy in the fourteenth century. Another famous bridge, known in the nursery song as the one where everyone dances, was built on arches across the turbulent Rhône (RONE) River at Avignon.

In the old vineyards of southern France, the harvest is celebrated with ancient dances.

RESORT AT CANNES: FASHIONABLE MOORING

O NE of the most colorful regions in France is Provence. Its Mediterranean coast, known as the Côte d'Azur (*coat da-*ZOOR), has for many years been a fabled land of pleasure.

The blue water of the busy harbor at Cannes (CAN) is ringed by the old section of town. Beyond the harbor the famous Boulevard de la Croisette (*krwah-*ZETT) runs parallel to the strip of beach where the wealthy and beautiful bare themselves to the Mediterranean sun. The great white luxury hotels, the casino, the palm trees and flowers, and the villas perched on the green hills are all part of fashionable Cannes. But this little harbor still retains the look of the simple fishing village from which the elegant resort sprang. The yacht in the background is the only new note.

In 1834 a cholera epidemic swept through France. That was the year that the British Chancellor, Lord Brougham (who gave his name to a

Great luxury superimposed on natural beauty— that is Eden Roc on the Riviera.

smart carriage), decided to winter in Nice, as was his custom. But because of the epidemic Nice was closed to foreign travelers. Lord Brougham angrily retraced his course along the Riviera coast and decided to stop at the small fishing village of Cannes. And just for spite he gave it his stamp of approval and his fashionable blessing. It now surpasses Nice as a luxury resort.

BATHING ON THE RIVIERA: NICE

WE ARE in Nice, and after looking at this view, can you think of a better place to be? The travel posters have not exaggerated the blue of the water or the brilliance of the colors. There is some alchemy of air and sunlight that makes color more vivid in this part of France. That is probably why so many of her great painters—Renoir (*ren*-WAHR), Picasso, Matisse, to name a few—have chosen to live and paint on the Riviera.

Nice is the capital of the Côte d'Azur, and it is situated on the Bay of the Angels. Two hundred years ago it was a rather dirty and indolent Mediterranean town. It was "discovered" as a winter resort by English tourists escaping from their miserable northern climate. Now Nice is a modern resort superimposed on the old harbor town.

Back in 1822 one of the earliest public works programs in history was initiated in Nice. The British colony here, killing two birds with one franc, set all the beggars and unemployed to work widening and paving the little seaside path. It has become one of the most famous and beautiful promenades in the world, with palm trees planted in its center and broad sidewalks running alongside. In honor of the British it is called the Promenade des Anglais (*pro-men*-AHD *daze ahng*-LAY).

Cannes is a more fashionable resort than Nice today, though no more beautiful. Saint-Raphaël attracts those happy addicts of "camping-out," and their tents can be seen along its stretches of beach. Monte Carlo is famous for its casino and its sun. And for those whose hearts warm to the landscape of Provence there are the inland towns, like Grasse.

CARNIVAL AT NICE: FEBRUARY FROLIC

EVERY year just before Lent the city of Nice cuts loose with one of the gayest, most colorful carnivals in the world. Lasting for several days, the festival is an elaborate one with music and fireworks, gorgeous floral displays, and parades of floats and grotesque papier-mâché figures like the one we see here.

The history of the carnival goes way back to the pagan festivals in ancient Greece when the people paid homage to their gods represented by masked men and women. The Romans adopted these celebrations to give a rousing welcome to the spring season, and when they colonized Gaul they introduced the custom there. Later the Christian church tried to put an end to the heathen merrymaking, but church authorities made little headway against the jovial temperament of the Mediterranean peoples. Finally, the festival was accepted and placed on the calendar just prior to the religious observance of Lent.

The word "carnival" comes from the Latin *carne vale*, which means "O flesh, farewell!" The Nice carnival ends the evening before Ash Wednesday, on Shrove Tuesday, which the French call "Fat Tuesday," or *Mardi gras*. The French settlers of Louisiana carried the celebration across the sea where it thrives today in New Orleans' famous Mardi gras. In Nice the carnival bursts into full glory for several days each February, but behind the scenes it is a year-round activity. There is an entire industry made up of *carnivaliers*, those craftsmen and workmen who design and build the carnival. It takes months to put this fantastic show together, and months to dismantle and store the paraphernalia. Then it is time to begin again.

The holiday throngs who crowd into Nice at the height of the season feel that the jollity and merrymaking are completely spontaneous. And in a way, in spite of the elaborate preparations made for it, the carnival at Nice is a colorful explosion of gaiety that springs quite naturally from the spirited people of this sun-drenched coast.

70

FLOWER FIELDS AT GRASSE: PERFUME HARVEST

LEAVING the seashore at Cannes we travel inland and up into the hills near Grasse (GRAHSS). The town is built on the side of a mountain about one thousand feet above a hollow that brims with flower beds and orange trees. Perfume begins with part of the enormous crop of flowers being harvested. These people are gathering roses, full blown and fragrant.

The air for miles around Grasse is perfumed with the scent of millions of flowers—carnations, lilies, mimosa—all cultivated for odor rather than appearance. Grasse is the perfume center of France, and to say that is the same as saying that Grasse is the perfume capital of the world. France's pre-eminence in the luxury trades—wine, perfume, silk, couture—is no accident. In a country devoted to beautiful living, the products of elegance would come first.

One reason for the popularity of French perfumes is that they are for the most part natural perfumes. They are created from the oils of flowers rather than from synthetics. In Grasse the great perfume factories cultivate fields of flowers, and literally millions of them must be crushed in order to extract even a small amount of oil. Perfume making is, in its way, as delicate a business as the making of wine. And, like wine making, the perfume industry is big business in France.

This vat of rose petals will be reduced to a small flask of absolute essence.

SNOWCLAD MEGEVE:
SKIERS PARADISE

MOVING northward from sunny Provence we find ourselves in the province of Savoy, whose eastern borders touch Italy and Switzerland. Within two hundred miles of the Riviera there are mountains and snow.

We have now traded the sunny south for the cool, sunny north and are high in the French Alps at the famous ski resort of Mégève (*may-*ZHEV).

This little town at the foot of Mont Joly (MON *zho-*LEE) was originally a quiet summer resort. Now, when the snow frosts the jagged mountain peaks, winter-sports enthusiasts cram the chalets and hotels. The French Ski School is located here, and the glittering white slopes teem with skiers hurtling down the mountainside in a spray of powdery snow. We have caught the skiers in a less athletic moment, taking their ease on this gay terrace, and enjoying the view they can't see when they are skiing on it. For some people this is the best part of the sport.

The Gothic majesty of Reims reminds us that the kings of France were crowned here.

Grenoble (*greh-*NO-*bl*), not far from Mégève, is the capital of the French Alps. It is a highly civilized university city and an important industrial center. Paper and gloves, two products France excels at making, have their chief factories here. In the mountains that ring Grenoble the monastery of La Grande Chartreuse (*lah grahnd shar-*TRUZE) has its amazing citadel cut into the rock. Here in these lonely heights the monks originated the jeweled yellow and green liqueurs that the province exports.

74

CHAMPAGNE CELLARS: TREASURY OF REIMS

THE monks at the monastery of La Grande Chartreuse weren't the only ones to experiment with spirits while following the spiritual life. Way up to the northeast, not far from Paris, a seventeenth-century monk named Dom Pérignon (*duhm pay-ree*-NYON) invented the drink that has become a symbol of France—champagne. This sparkling white wine is made only from grapes grown in the old province of Champagne, and most particularly from around Reims and Epernay (*ay-pair*-NAY).

In this picture you see one of the cool, dry chalk caverns under the city of Reims. These were once chalk quarries, but now they are the even-temperated cellars so necessary to the maturing of the delicate wine. In World War I, when Reims' beautiful coronation cathedral was nearly destroyed by bombardment, these cellars became an underground city with churches, courts, schools and living accommodations for 20,000 people.

The province of Champagne has a long and interesting history. The building of the cathedral in Reims was begun in 1211 and it was, for many years, the site of coronation ceremonies for the kings of France.

This province was situated so that during the middle ages it was at a crossing of the roads between Germany, Italy and Flanders. The area became famous for its month-long fairs. Furs, linens, spices, fine tapestries, metal work, leather goods, all poured into the province and were exchanged at the fairs. For centuries Champagne was a center for producing woolen goods. The fine wool was carded, spun and woven into woolen cloth.

Now, just as each province of France is known for certain foods, so is Champagne. Near a great northern forest, the area is famous for its special ways of serving game. Meat in general is excellent. Veal and lamb is roasted and served with a sauce made of lettuce, carrots and cabbage. Red cabbage soup is a specialty of the region. And the spiced bread of Reims and the rich cookies found there are unusual and delicious.

CASTLE OF ROMANCE: LOIRE VALLEY

THE proverbial castles in Spain are daydreams, but castles in France really exist —probably in greater numbers and variety than anywhere else in the world. From Richard the Lionhearted's grim dungeon to splendid Versailles, they tell the story of the country's slow climb from the dark centuries of violence to the bright era of the Sun King's courtly magnificence.

Originally a castle was a fortress, built for protection, with massive walls, mighty towers and a moat. But by the fifteenth century things were settling down, and people could dare to build castles in a homier style. The romantic picture we are looking at now shows the Château du Moulin (*shah*-TOE *du moo*-LAN) in the Loire Valley. Built in the late fifteenth century it reflects the charm and graciousness that were beginning to temper the austere Norman keeps and battlements of a less placid time. France was already cultivating the art of living.

The Loire Valley was to early France what the Riviera is today— the playground of the wealthy. In this warm and pleasant valley the fabulous pleasure palaces of the French kings still stand, their Renaissance elegance mirrored in country river or quiet lake. These are the lovely and romantic monuments of a highly civilized country. They retain the essence of France.

In France the humblest peasant knows that a man's house is his castle.

SOME IMPORTANT DATES IN FRENCH HISTORY

c. 600 B.C. *Phocaean Greeks from Asia Minor establish the town of Marseilles in Southeast France on the Gulf of Lions.*

52 B.C. *Julius Caesar conquers the Gauls in battle of Alesia near Dijon. Gaul becomes Roman province.*

451 *Battle of Châlons. Franks and Visigoths combine to repel invasion of Attila the Hun. Franks unite country, named France.*

784-814 *Reign of Charlemagne, son of Pepin. Greatest figure to rise out of wreckage of Roman Empire. Crowned Emperor of the West in St. Peter's, Rome, on Christmas Day 800.*

843 *Treaty of Verdun, tripartite agreement between three grandsons of Charlemagne. Divides empire of Charlemagne into what is to become Germany and France.*

850 *Beginning of the Norse invasions. Province of Normandy founded, 924.*

987 *Hugh Capet, Duke of Paris, unifies France; makes Paris capital of small nation. Dynasty rules until 1328.*

1066 *William, Duke of Normandy, conquers England.*

1429 *Joan of Arc leads French army and raises siege of Orléans. Has Charles VII crowned at Reims. Wounded in the siege of Paris. Captured at Compiègne by Burgundians and turned over to British; burned at stake in 1431.*

1598 *Henry (IV) of Navarre, first of Bourbon line, grants a measure of religious freedom to Protestant Huguenots in Edict of Nantes.*

1643-1715 *72-year reign of Louis XIV, self-titled "Sun King."*

1789-1794 *French Revolution begins July 14. King and Queen, "Citizen and Citizeness Capet," guillotined in the Place de la Révolution (now the Place de la Concorde). The Revolution turns into "Reign of Terror."*

1804-1815 *The First Empire under Napoleon Bonaparte. Ends with defeat at Waterloo by British. Napoleon exiled to Elba.*

1815-1848 *Restoration of the monarchy under Louis XVIII, Charles X and Louis-Philippe.*

1852-1870 *The Second Empire under Napoleon III.*

1870-1871 *Franco-Prussian War culminates in Treaty of Frankfurt, which leaves Empire bankrupt.*

1875-1946 *The Third Republic is established. Leads France through events of World Wars I and II.*

1946-1958 *Fourth Republic, headed by numerous Premiers, ends in political and economic chaos.*

Dec. 1, 1958 *Charles de Gaulle is elected President of the Fifth French Republic.*

SOME FAMOUS NAMES IN FRENCH HISTORY

VERCINGETORIX (died c. 46 B.C.)—*Leader of the Gauls in the battle against the Roman legions. Defeated by Julius Caesar at Alesia.*

CHARLEMAGNE (742-814)—*Greatest Carolingian king, united much of Europe through conquest. Glorified in "The Song of Roland."*

WILLIAM THE CONQUEROR (1027-1087)—*Duke of Normandy, later King of England. Pivotal figure in European history; brought influence and culture of the Continent, especially France, to England.*

JOAN OF ARC (1412?-1431)—*Urged by heavenly voices, Maid of Orléans went to the aid of the French Dauphin and prevented the English from overrunning France.*

LOUIS XIV (1638-1715)—*The "Sun King," built Versailles, encouraged the arts and the theater—playwrights Molière, Racine and Corneille frequented his court.*

MOLIERE (1622-1673)—*Pseudonym of Jean Baptiste Poquelin, dramatist, actor, master of comedy. Wrote "The Misanthrope," and "The Doctor in Spite of Himself."*

MANSART, FRANCOIS (1598-1666) and MANSART, JULES HARDOUIN (1646-1708)—*Greatest architects of Renaissance period in France. François gave his name to "mansard roof," which he used frequently. Jules was responsible for much of Palace of Versailles, including the Hall of Mirrors.*

VOLTAIRE (1694-1778)—*Assumed name of François Arouet, philosopher and author, renowned for his biting wit exemplified in the novel "Candide."*

ROUSSEAU, JEAN-JACQUES (1712-1778)—*Philosopher, author, political theorist. Maintained man was good by nature and had been corrupted by civilization, advocated "return to nature." His works "Social Contract" and "Confessions" had great influence on pre-Revolutionary French thought.*

ROBESPIERRE, MAXIMILIEN MARIE (1758-1794)—*One of the leaders of the French Revolution, known as "the Incorruptible." Partially responsible for the "Reign of Terror," which ended when he himself was guillotined.*

LAFAYETTE, MARQUIS de (1757-1834)—*Soldier, statesman, democratic aristocrat. Played an important role as a general in the American Revolution. Returned to France to fight for democratic monarchy.*

NAPOLEON BONAPARTE (1769-1821)—*Emperor of France. Brilliant victories as a general under leaders of Revolution made him a hero. Appointed Minister of War under the Directory. In 1799, coup d'état ended Directory; Napoleon became First Consul. In 1804 crowned himself Emperor. Invasion of Russia marked beginning of his decline; battle against British at Waterloo marked the end. Died in exile on the island of St. Helena in 1821. Remains buried in Les Invalides, Paris.*

HUGO, VICTOR MARIE (1802-1885)—*Poet, dramatist, novelist; France's leading exponent of Romanticism. Memorialized the conditions in pre-Revolutionary France in "Les Misérables."*

PASTEUR, LOUIS (1822-1895)—*Chemist, best known for his experiments that led to the process of pasteurization of milk, also developed vaccines to prevent anthrax and hydrophobia.*

CEZANNE, PAUL (1839-1906)—*French Impressionist painter, studied with Pissarro, worked with and influenced such great artists as Manet, Monet, and the Dutch post-Impressionist Van Gogh. Known for brilliant landscapes of native Provence.*

CURIE, MARIE SKLODOWSKA (1867-1934)—*Chemist and physicist, who with her husband, Pierre, discovered polonium and radium, pioneered in the field of radioactivity. First to win two Nobel Prizes.*

SARTRE, JEAN-PAUL (1905-   )—*Philosopher and writer, founder of the Existentialist movement that has pervaded French philosophy since the end of World War II.*

DE GAULLE, CHARLES (1890-   )—*President of France's Fifth Republic.*

SOME FRENCH WORDS AND PHRASES

Here is a list of words and phrases that would be useful to know when traveling in France. The words are given in English and French and then in simple phonetics with the accented syllable in small capitals. "Bonne chance!"—which means "Good luck!"

Do you speak English? — Parlez-vous Anglais? (*par-lay*-voo ZAHN-*gleh*)
How do you say . . . ? — Comment dit-on . . . ? (*koh-mahn dee*-TOHN . . .)
I don't understand. — Je ne comprends pas. (*zhuh nuh* KOM-*pran* PA)
What do you want? — Que voulez-vous? (KUH *voo-lay*-VOO)
Where is . . . ? — Où est . . . ? (*oo* EH)
How far? — A quelle distance? (*ah kehl dees*-TAHNS)
How long? (time) — Combien de temps? (*kohm-byen duh* TAHN)
How? — Comment? (*koh*-MAHN)
How much is it? — Combien est-ce? (*kohm-byen* EHSS)
Who? What? — Qui? (KEE) Quoi? (KWAH)
When? Why? — Quand? (KAHN) Pourquoi? (*poor*-KWAH)
Please. — S'il vous plaît. (*seel voo* PLEH)
Thank you very much. — Merci beaucoup. (*mehr-see boh*-KOO)
Excuse me (or pardon). — Excusez-moi. (*ehx-kew-say*-MWAH)
Can you help me? — Pouvez-vous m'aider? (*poo-vay-voo meh*-DAY)
Yes. No. — Oui (WEE) Non (NOHN)
Perhaps. — Peut-être (*puh*-TEH-*truh*)
Enough. Too much. — Assez (*ah*-SAY) Trop (TROH)
Much (or many). — Beaucoup (*boh*-KOO)
Good. Better. — Bien (BYEN) Mieux (MYUH)
Bad. Worse. — Mal (MAHL) Pire (PEER)
Now. Later. — Maintenant (*mant*-NAHN) Plus tard (*plew* TAHR)
Near (to). Far (from). — Près de (PREH *duh*) Loin de (LWAN *duh*)
Here. There. — Ici (*ee*-SEE) Là (LAH)
Hello (Good day). — Bonjour (*bohn*-ZHOOR)
Good-by. — Au revoir (*oh* VWAHR)
Airplane. Airport. — Avion (*ah-vee*-OHN) L'aéroport (*lay-roh*-POHR)
Train. Railroad Station. — Train (TRAN) La gare (*lah* GAR)
Bus. Boat. — Autobus (*oh-toe*-BEWSS) Bateau (*bah*-TOE)
Ticket. Ticket Office. — Un billet (UHN *bee*-YEH) Le guichet (*luh ghee*-SHEH)
Hotel. Room. — L'hôtel (*loh*-TEHL) Une chambre (*ewhn* SHAWM-*bruh*)
Men's Room — Ladies' Room. — La Toilette (*lah twah*-LEHT)

NUMBERS

One	Un (UHN)
Two	Deux (DUH)
Three	Trois (TRWAH)
Four	Quatre (KAH-*truh*)
Five	Cinq (SANK)
Six	Six (SEESS)
Seven	Sept (SEHT)
Eight	Huit (HWEET)
Nine	Neuf (NUHF)
Ten	Dix (DEESS)
One hundred	Cent (SAHN)
One thousand	Mille (MEEL)

DAYS OF THE WEEK

Sunday	Dimanche (*dee*-MAHNSH)
Monday	Lundi (LUHN-*dee*)
Tuesday	Mardi (MAR-*dee*)
Wednesday	Mercredi (MEHR-*kruh-dee*)
Thursday	Jeudi (ZHUH-*dee*)
Friday	Vendredi (VAHN-*druh-dee*)
Saturday	Samedi (SAM-*dee*)
Day	Jour (ZHOOR)
Week	Semaine (*s'*MEN)
Month	Mois (MWAH)
Year	Année (*an*-NAY)
Hour	Heure (UHR)
Today	Aujourd'hui (*oh-zhoor*-DWEE)
Yesterday	Hier (YEHR)

MONEY

Franc (FRAHN)
Centime (*sahn*-TEEM) 100 centimes to the franc

INDEX

84